Dealing With Depression

Dealing With Depression
By Sue Savage

Copyright 2015 by The Choice is Yours Counseling, LLC

All rights reserved under the Pan-American and International Copyrights Conventions.
This book may not be reproduced, in whole or part, in any form or by any means electronic or mechanical, including photocopying, recording, or by any informational storage retrieval system known or hereafter invented, without permission from The Choice is Yours Counseling, LLC

Cover & Layout Design: Aria Creative/www.aria-creative.com

Library of Congress Cataloging-in-Publication Available upon request
ISBN: 978-1-4951-6802-4

Contents

Group 1: Purpose, Rules, and Understanding Depression
Group Purpose ... 5
Group Rules ... 6
Poem: Listen ... 7
Assertive Bill of Rights ... 8
Sad, Depressed, or Clinically Depressed? ... 9
Assessments for Depression ... 10
Symptoms of Depression ... 11
Different Types of Depression ... 12
Group Exercise 1: Your Depression ... 13
Group Exercise 2: Depression Collage ... 13

Group 2: A Closer Look at Depression
Who Gets Depressed? ... 14
What Causes Depression? ... 14
Myths About Depression ... 15
Mental Health Providers ... 16
Your Treatment Plan ... 17
Group Exercise 1: Depression Myths ... 18
Group Exercise 2: Your Treatment Plan ... 18

Group 3: Common Treatment Options
Exercising ... 19
Counseling ... 20
Antidepressants ... 20
Alternative Herbal Supplements ... 21
Nutrition ... 21
Self-Care ... 21
Support Groups ... 22
Meditation ... 22
Spirituality ... 22
Group Exercise 1: Your Self-care plan ... 23
Group Exercise 2: Mind Body Spirit Connection ... 23

Contents

Group 4: Living With Depression
The Stigma of Depression 24
Societal Expectations 24
Self-Expectations 25
Family Expectations 25
Friend Expectations 25
Group Exercise 1: Stigmas 26
Group Exercise 2: Changing the Future 26

Group 5: Depression and Life Events
Major Events 27
Staying Stuck Can Feed Depression 28
Organizations to Get to Know 29
Group Exercise 1: Feeling Stuck 30
Group Exercise 2: Depression Timeline 30

Group 6: Meditation and Depression
Learning to Be Mindful 31
Practicing Being Mindful 32
Mind-Body Connection 32
Body Scan 33
Group Exercise 1: Body Scan and Visualization 34
Group Exercise 2: Mindfulness Meditation 34
Closing Thoughts 35
Your Closing Thoughts 36
References 37

Welcome...

to a group where you can explore and learn more about your depression. Depression can make you feel like you're all on your own to face the world. Connecting with others who "get what you're going through" can be one of the most helpful things you ever do. Whether you've just been diagnosed with depression or you've had bouts for years and just want to gain a deeper understanding of it, this group is for you.

This group will provide you with a safe and accepting place to receive encouragement, share coping skills, exchange ideas, and give you the assurance that someone else knows what you are going through. We will look more closely at what depression is, how it's treated, what medication can and cannot do, meditation and depression, and work together on some exercises.

Depression is the leading cause of disability worldwide and is a major contributor to the global burden of disease.
- World Health Organization -

Group 1:
Purpose, Rules, and Understanding Depression

Group members will support one another as we progress toward a better understanding of depression. Sharing your experiences with depression can release feelings in you and perhaps someone else in the group. That's OK, as we are here for one another. There is power in group support and I encourage you to participate as much as you choose. When anyone is sharing two things are extremely important: there is to be no judgment passed and what is shared in the group, stays in the group.

> *"Depression is a flaw in chemistry, not character"*
> – Healthyplace.com –

Group Rules

Confidentiality... what goes on in the group, stays in the group. Who is attending the group and what is shared should not be discussed with anyone else.

Exceptions to Confidentiality ... the group leader is required by law to report child abuse and elder abuse, as well as knowledge of you or another being at risk for harm.

Consistency of Attendance- is Expected. Group cohesion is only possible in the context of regular attendance.

Punctuality is Expected and Appreciated... arriving late is disrespectful to the other members of the group.

Take Personal Responsibility... this will help you get the most out of your time in the group. This means pace your sharing according to what you feel comfortable with (building trust and taking risks). Asking for what you need/want from the group. Practicing boundaries when appropriate. Claiming time to talk. Saying no to other group member's questions or requests that make you feel uncomfortable.

Respect Other Group Members... by letting each person speak her thoughts, feelings, experiences for herself. No interrupting or helping others finish sharing their thoughts or feelings. You can non-judgmentally respond to what is being shared, but NO advice is to be given.

Respecting Other Group Members... by asking for and receiving permission from another before any personal touch such as giving a hug.

Tolerance- practice tolerance for opinions and beliefs that may differ from yours.

Practice Using I Statements... when sharing or responding to another group member's sharing.

Taking Care of Yourself... if something difficult comes up for you in the group and you would like to talk about it in individual counseling , see your group leader.

Poem

Listen
Anonymous

When I ask you to listen to me
And you start giving me advice,
You haven't done what I've asked.

When I ask you to listen to me
And you begin to tell me why I shouldn't feel that way
You are trampling on my feelings.

When I ask you to listen to me
And you feel like you have to do something to solve my problems,
You've failed me … as strange as that my sound.

Advice is cheap: go on-line and read Dear Abby or many others.
And I can do for myself: I'm not helpless
Maybe discouraged and faltering a little, but not helpless
When you do something I can do for myself, you contribute to my fears.

When you accept that I feel what I feel, no matter how irrational, then I can quit trying to convince you and get about the business of understanding what is behind my irrational feelings. And when I can do that, the answers are obvious and I can follow my heart instead of your advice.

So please, listen and just hear me. And, if you want to talk, wait a minute for your turn, and I will quietly listen to you.

Assertive Bill of Rights
Anonymous

I HAVE THE RIGHT TO…….

- accept and respect myself and others
- experience and express my feelings
- say no and not feel guilty
- my dignity
- slow down and think before I act
- change my mind
- make mistakes
- be responsible for my own life
- feel good about myself
- have my own beliefs, ideas and values without apology to anyone
- take care of my whole being: body , mind, and spirit
- tell others how I want to be treated
- ask for information
- have healthy, life-enhancing relationships.

Group 1:
Sad, Depressed, or Clinically Depressed?

SADNESS

Sadness and depression are not the same things. The words should not be used interchangeably, as doing so minimizes clinical depression. Words that can be used interchangeably with sadness are grief, heartache, sorrow, disappointment, unhappiness, and mourning. Sadness is generally related to loss. The loss of something you held very dear.

The confusion between sadness and depression is reflective of the fact that sadness can be a symptom of depression. And note the words can be, as some do not even experience sadness as a symptom. Sadness as a symptom has to linger and last for 2 weeks or more to qualify as a symptom of depression. If sadness persists and is also accompanied by other symptoms of depression then it may be more than just normal sadness.

SITUATIONAL

Situational, or what some refer to as a garden-variety, depression shares common symptoms with clinical depression. Situational depression is tied to a recent event which you are having a hard time adjusting to. It could be financial stress, job loss, retirement, and numerous other major life events. Situational depression symptoms can also include crying, sadness, worry, anxiety, increased use of alcohol and drugs, and many others. Situational depression can even be accompanied by headaches, stomach aches, and other physical symptoms. The depressive feelings and symptoms related to your particular event, however, usually subside as you adjust to whatever the troubling circumstances are.

CLINICAL DEPRESSION

Clinical depression can appear for no apparent reason, as well as be attached to a recent change of events in your life. Or sometimes a major life event will trigger the onset of a bout of depression. There is also oftentimes a family history of depression with those who suffer from clinical depression. Another symptom that differentiates the two is that clinical depression is more likely to be accompanied by thoughts and attempts of suicide. Since the basis of clinical depression is brain chemistry imbalance, whether or not you respond to an antidepressant is also considered a clue to having clinical depression.

Group 1:
Assessments for Depression

To distinguish the type and severity of your depression, you can take an assessment. This series of questions ask you about your mood and feelings surrounding the last week or so. Many health insurance companies provide clinicians with depression assessment tools for their clients. Clients can take the results of their test to their primary care physician or psychiatrist and begin to talk about the value and risks of going on an antidepressant.

Assessments are also valuable as they can be retaken periodically to see how your treatment is progressing. Do you recall the initial assessment your health care provider used to assess your depression? Did your health care professional retest you as your treatment progressed?

Group 1:
Symptoms of Depression

_____ Feeling persistent emptiness

_____ Crying easily

_____ Preoccupation with unrealistic expectations, worry, feelings of failure

_____ Loss of interest in things that generally bring you pleasure

_____ Sleeping too much or too little

_____ Feeling guilty, hopeless, or not worth anything

_____ Tired every day

_____ Gaining or losing weight

_____ Difficulty remembering things or concentrating on things that need to be done

_____ Feeling like nothing in life matters

_____ Losing self-confidence and feeling useless

_____ Isolating – avoiding other people

_____ Feeling like you just can't even get out of bed

_____ Feeling like nothing is going to make you feel any better

_____ Thoughts of suicide

_____ Recurring thoughts of suicide

_____ Imagining or devising a plan for suicide

_____ Suicide attempts

GatheringForGroups.com

Group 1:
Different Types of Depression

There are different diagnoses for depression. The symptoms you may be experiencing can range in intensity from mild to moderate to severe. Here are some common forms of depression:

MAJOR DEPRESSIVE DISORDER: persistent feelings of deep sadness for more than 2 weeks-the sadness cannot be due to medical conditions or substance abuse problems. Symptoms can include decreased physical and social ability to function on a daily basis that reflects a decline from previous daily functioning. The duration of a bout of depression can last from 2 weeks-2 months.

DYSTHMIA: or as it is now referred to as persistent depressive disorder. Dysthmia is a chronic depression that is present most days over a period of 2 years. With dysthmia there are generally more prevalent cognitive symptoms (low-self-esteem, negative core beliefs, etc) present.

SAD OR SEASONAL AFFECTIVE DISORDER: is a form of depression that accompanies a change in the seasons. It is more prevalent in the fall and winter months and is much more than just the winter blues. Bright light has been shown to affect our brain chemistry. People with SAD experience mood changes, sleeping too much, and other symptoms that are common with major depression. These symptoms interfere with your daily ability to function. Light therapy is an available treatment option.

PREMENSTRUAL DYSPHORIC DISORDER: these are depressive symptoms that can accompany hormonal changes that begin a week before your period and improve a few days after your period. Symptoms include depressed mood, self-deprecating remarks, anxiety, changes in appetite, and sleep. These symptoms follow a predictable and cyclic pattern around that time of the month.

POST- PARTUM DEPRESSION: this type of depression affects 10-15% of women shortly after childbirth. This severely depressed mood usually appears 4 weeks or later after the baby is born. Symptoms include crying spells, insomnia, depressed mood, anxiety, lack of concentration, and demeaning thoughts. This depression can affect the mom and her ability to tend to her baby's needs.

■ **GROUP EXERCISE 1**
Your depression - describe what it feels and looks like when you're depressed.

_____

_____

_____

■ **GROUP EXERCISE 2**
Depression Collage

_____

_____

_____

> *" That is all I want in life:*
> *for this pain to seem purposeful"*
>
> - Elizabeth Wurtzel -

Group 2:
A Closer Look at Depression

WHO GETS DEPRESSED?
Every year, about 1 in 10 people, more women than men, experience bouts of depression. Depression can happen to anyone, at any age. According to the Huffington Post (2015) 11% of the number of people globally are affected by some form of depression. Seventy percent of adolescents have some type of depressive disorder by age 18. The percentage of women who suffer from post-partum depression is around 30%. According to a 2010 CDC report, HALF of all ambulatory care visits had the primary diagnosis of major depressive disorder.

WHAT CAUSES DEPRESSION?
Although breakthroughs in understanding the causes of depression are continuing to be made, the reality is researchers still don't know the exact causes. They do have these possibilities to offer:

- Differences in brain chemistry - brain chemicals (neurotransmitters) are naturally occurring substances researchers think play a role in affecting a person's mood. When these chemicals are out of balance the result may be depression.
- Biological predisposition - like so many things we inherit, depression appears to be more common in families who carry the trait. This predisposition only mildly increases, not guarantees, your chances of having depression.
- Traumatic life events and/or traumatic events in childhood are thought to have an effect on developing brain chemistry. Research also points to developmental trauma which is growing up in a home where abuse and addiction are present.
- Nutrition- it's no secret that the foods we eat have an impact on our mood. Many doctors are now pointing toward deficiencies in Vitamin D and B-12 as suspects in depression.
- Thyroid disorders - anyone suffering from depression needs to have their doctor evaluate the role their thyroid may be playing. This is a very important, often overlooked contributor to depression.
- Certain medications can increase your risk of depression.
- Substance abuse - a high percentage of substance abusers also experience depression.

Group 2:
Myths about Depression

When science doesn't definitively understand something, people create myths. These myths perpetuate misinformation and often scare people away from getting the help they need. Let's debunk some of the more common myths surrounding depression.

MYTH #1 Depression is all in your head. You can snap out of it if you want to.
No one chooses depression and no one has the ability to snap out of it.
Our mind-body-spirit are all connected and depression generally affects them all.

MYTH #2 Having depression is a real sign of weakness.
This myth centers around the fact that women are twice as likely to suffer from depression as men. The myth is perpetuated by those who continue to think men are more emotionally strong than women.

MYTH #3 Antidepressants just numb me out.
Antidepressants work by lifting your mood, not by taking you down further or taking away any of your feelings. It's the depression making you feel numb.

MYTH #4 Men don't get depressed.
Men are reluctant to get help for their depression, due to the stigma that it makes them appear weaker in their ability to handle life. Depression is an illness, not a weakness.

MYTH #5 An antidepressant is all you need to feel better.
Wouldn't that be nice? While an antidepressant is often helpful in lifting your mood, much more can be gained by looking at the broader picture which includes your nutrition and getting counseling. Your improved mood can give you a better perspective from which to make decisions regarding your treatment.

MYTH #6 Antidepressants are addictive.
Antidepressants are NOT addictive. The medical definition of addictive is that you have to take more and more to achieve the same effects. What you can experience, however, (if you stop taking them cold turkey) is what doctors call discontinuation symptoms. Tapering down as you get off your antidepressants will reduce and/or eliminate these symptoms.

MYTH #7 Teens with depression are the highest risk group for suicide.
Teens are a very high risk group. Teen suicides tend to make it in the news more often than the highest group at risk, which is elderly white males.

Group 2:
Mental Health Providers

Sometimes there is confusion over which healthcare provider does what when you are seeking help with your depression. Let's take a brief look at the different roles these different mental health professionals provide:

Psychiatrist: a psychiatrist is an MD who specializes in the prevention and treatment of mental illness. Psychiatrist do psychiatric evaluations and can prescribe medication. They are in network with many health insurances.

Psychologist: has a PhD in Psychology, can conduct different tests (IQ, personality, etc.) as well as do therapy. Psychologists are recognized by health insurance companies and are generally in network with them.

LCPC (licensed clinical professional counselor): has a Master Degree in Counseling and is licensed through the state. LCPCs are recognized by health insurance companies and are often in network.

LCSW (licensed clinical social worker): has a Masters Degree in Social Work and is licensed by the state. LCSWs are also recognized by health insurance companies and can be found in many provider networks.

When looking for your health care provider, make sure the individual has a state license and is in-network with your insurance plan. You can find this information on-line and/or through your insurance company.

Group 2:
Your Treatment Plan

Managing your depression is on-going. Form a partnership between your doctor, your counselor, your family, and your friends. Keep your local crisis hotline numbers on your cell phone. Continue treatment and don't give up. If you are on medication, stay on it until your doctor says otherwise. Talk to others about how they manage their depression.

Hotline number _____

Take good care of yourself when you're depressed. Remember it is important to get plenty of exercise and rest and maintain good nutritional habits. Hang around encouraging people who are there to support you and help meet your needs during your depression.

Simplify your life when you are feeling depressed. It's OK to turn down plans with people or not feel up to being a part of something you usually participate in.

■ **GROUP EXERCISE 1**
Depression Myths – What myths have you heard about depression?

_____

_____

_____

■ **GROUP EXERCISE 2**
Your Treatment Plan

_____

_____

_____

> *It's so difficult to describe depression to someone who's never been there, because it is not sadness. I know sadness. Sadness is to feel and cry. But it's that cold absence of feeling—that really hollowed out feeling.*
>
> - J.K. Rowling -

Group 3:
Common Treatment Options

There is no "one-size fits all" recommended treatment for clinical depression. What works for one person, may or may not work for another. Common forms of treatment include therapy, medication, and lifestyle changes and/or a combination approach. Each one and each combination takes time and commitment to try and evaluate whether or not it is right for you. When designing your treatment plan, always consider

- Who is needed on your treatment team
- Are your providers covered in-network by your health insurance
- How long the treatment may take
- What role your family and friends will play
- If taking medication - what the possible risks and benefits are
- How much will it cost
- Are there any side effects and, if so, how long will they probably last
- The length of commitment needed to see results

EXERCISING
Regular exercise has been shown to have benefits for everyone of all ages. Getting out and exercising becomes even more important as part of your day when you are depressed. Exercise boosts your serotonin, which in turn boosts you mood. It can also help you sleep better.

Your exercise plan doesn't have to resemble someone who is training for a 10 k race. It can be as simple as briskly walking for 30 minutes a day around your neighborhood. If you are not used to exercising, start slowly and each week add some more time to your walk. Prior to exercising, seek some good advice from your physician about where to start and how to progress with your plan.

Group 3:
Common Treatment Options (Cont...)

COUNSELING

There are many kinds of counseling for different kinds of issues. A form of counseling known as CBT or Cognitive Behavioral Therapy is often a recommended form of therapy to do with someone with depression. Simply stated, the therapist works with you to change unhelpful negative thoughts, beliefs, and behaviors. According to Beck, the depression prone person possesses negative beliefs, a negative view of themselves (seeing themselves as worthless, unlovable and so forth), and sees their environment as overwhelming and filled with obstacles and failures. They see their future as hopeless and believe that no amount of work on their part is going to change that.

Therapy can help by giving you new coping skills for dealing with your depression. You can learn to set healthy boundaries, explore your negative thinking patterns, gain insights into any underlying problems, and benefit from having someone to lend an empathetic ear to how you are doing.

ANTIDEPRESSANTS

If you watch TV, you'll soon notice that antidepressants are a highly advertised form of treatment for depression. New drugs are introduced via cartoons or actors. The drug's side-effects are quickly rattled off as you watch someone becoming happier by the end of the commercial, thanks to their medication.

The theory is that antidepressants act on the chemical pathways of your brain related to your moods. Antidepressants are drugs which alter the body's chemistry, specifically at the cellular level of the nervous system. Neurotransmitters (the chemicals that need to be present to pass along a nervous signal from cell to cell) are specialized hormones. Most of the body's neurotransmitters are produced in the stomach which makes appetite and GI problems common side effects of taking antidepressants.

There are now many classes of antidepressants available to work on different neurotransmitters. Finding the right one or right mix of medications is an art and a science. Working closely with your doctor/psychiatrist will help you find the right medication(s) for you.

Group 3:
Common Treatment Options (Cont...)

ALTERNATIVE OR COMPLEMENTARY HERBAL SUPPLEMENTS
Research doesn't show much conclusive evidence that alternative treatments are as effective as antidepressants, except when it comes to milder forms of depression. There are a wide variety of herbal supplements available and the same caution should be taken using them, as when taking any antidepressant. Many supplements can interact and disable medications you are on and supplements generally have their side effects as well. You should always check with your doctor before taking any supplements. Herbal supplements are not monitored by the FDA which is another general concern surrounding their use.

NUTRITION
Studying the relationship between nutrition and the brain (nutritional neuroscience) is an emerging field. Nutritionist are evaluating the role of vitamin deficiencies, eating patterns, bad mood foods, and deficiencies/additions to your diet that could affect depression. Research on the nutritional mechanisms and their effect on the brain and nervous system is growing every day. The brain consumes an immense amount of energy, so the transfer of energy from foods to the nervous system is super important in controlling your brain function.

SELF-CARE
"You time" includes any activities or practices geared toward reducing your stress and increasing/enhancing your short and long-term well-being. "You time" is not selfish time, it is a must time!

Think of self-care as your active contribution to enhancing the quality of your physical, emotional, and spiritual well-being. Taking part in preventive medical screenings, eating healthy, exercising, getting enough sleep, laughing, releasing emotions, being in healthy relationships, enjoying life, and developing faith in spiritual pursuits are all examples of practicing good self-care.

GatheringForGroups.com

Group 3:
Common Treatment Options (Cont...)

SUPPORT GROUPS
There are many benefits to joining a support group. You don't have to feel alone in your efforts to manage your depression. You can learn new ideas from others, gather new information, share what is on your heart, and gain support from others who understand what it is like to deal with depression.

MEDITATION
Settling your mind down can boost your mood. Mindfulness meditation has been shown in some studies to alleviate symptoms of depression. Meditation is an approach to training your mind to slow down and to focus on staying in the present moment. Breathing and other techniques are easy-to-learn tools for clearing your mind. Researchers are now studying the effects of long-term, consistent meditation practices and the positive benefits on the brain.

Mindfulness meditation and its relationship to depression will be discussed more in Group 6.

SPIRITUALITY
Finding hope in a higher power, praying, sitting in silence, holding on to the belief things will get better, and many other aspects of spirituality can aid in helping you endure your depression. Exploring, holding on to, and finding comfort in one's spirituality can be an important piece of dealing with depression.

■ **GROUP EXERCISE 1:**
Your Self-care Plan

_____

_____

_____

■ **GROUP EXERCISE 2:**
Mind, body, spirit connection

_____

_____

_____

> *"It's a bit like walking down a long, dark corridor, never knowing when the light will go on."*
>
> — Neil Lennon —

Group 4:
Living with Depression

Experiencing a mood disorder can be painful enough, but the stigma attached can make it even worse. Instead of receiving the compassion and support you need during this time, shame can deter you from seeking help.

THE STIGMA OF DEPRESSION
Our culture has some fairly rigid cultural programming that defines how people feel about many things. Although our society is making strides in talking more openly about depression, there is still a lingering stigma surrounding depression.

A stigma is defined as when someone views you in a negative light because you have an issue that they don't. Their ignorance regarding that issue produces negative prejudices. These openly spoken or implied prejudices can often contribute to a person's sense of shame and self-doubt surrounding being depressed. Feeling stigmatized is dangerous as people will hide their suicidal thoughts from others instead of seeking help.

Depression's stigma also contributes to the expectations people form and the depressed individual develops.

SOCIETAL EXPECTATIONS
Some people are still living in fear of telling their employers that they missed work due to a bout of depression. They fear they will be looked at differently and/or their depression will not be accepted as a valid reason for being absent. Job discrimination for those who talk about their depression is always a possibility.

Some people still look down on people with depression stating that their depression is an excuse for being lazy or irresponsible. They believe that the person who has depression is weak and can snap out of it if they wanted to. The reality, however, is just the opposite - it takes a very strong person to navigate their way through a bout of depression.

Group 4:
Living with Depression (Cont...)

SELF-EXPECTATIONS

Every age group carries with it different self-expectations when it comes to dealing with depression. Some older people think they are too old to get help for depression. Men think they will be viewed as weak if they talk about it. Teens hide it to be cool and fit in instead of being different. Women can feel guilty for having it as they "should" be able to nurture their families without letting anything stand in their way.

Many people with depression expect their lives to carry on as usual. That's not going to happen. Try and tough it out as you may, treat yourself gently during these difficult times. Give yourself permission to slow down and not be involved in things that drain your energy or take your mood down further. There is no shame in saying no when you know you're just not up to participating in certain activities.

It's time to put your "shoulds", preconceived ideas, myths, and critical self-talk behind. Work toward accepting that life will not be the same when depression strikes.

FAMILY EXPECTATIONS

Ideally, your family would offer you unconditional love and support when you're suffering from depression. Many, however, are unfamiliar with what to do and leave you alone to deal with it yourself. Some families even have the unfair expectation that you will carry on as usual while you're depressed.

Educate your family members on depression and do what you can to explain how it is for you and what you need from them when you are depressed. Don't let their lack of support make you feel unimportant and add to your depressed feelings.

FRIEND EXPECTATIONS

Your close friends may or may not know how to support you during your depression. As with your family members, try and educate them when you are not depressed as to what your needs are during this time.

Friends will most likely express their concerns for you. Listen to them and try and consider what they are saying. Let them support you by accompanying you to the doctor, cooking for you, checking in on you, and other things that will be easier for you if you let someone help. Trust them when they feel you need more professional care, as they have your safety in mind as well.

■ **GROUP EXERCISE 1:**
Stigmas. Describe any sense of stigma that you have felt when you shared with someone that you have depression.

_____
_____
_____
_____
_____

■ **GROUP EXERCISE 2:**
Changing the Future — Making a " what it will take" collage depicting eliminating the stigma surrounding depression.

_____
_____
_____

"When you have depression simply existing is a full-time job."

- Healthyplace.com -

Group 5:
Depression and Life Events

A complex relationship exists between challenging life events and the onset of depression. Does the major life event trigger the onset of depression or does having depression make you more susceptible to having a harder time going through major life events? The only professional agreement when answering that question is that it takes a major triggering event in someone's life who is already prone to depression to initiate the first episode. And there is a theory, known as the kindling effect, that states the initial episode of depression sparks changes in your brain chemistry making you more prone to future episodes.

Here's a list of common major events. The list is not complete by any means.
- Divorce
- Moving
- Job loss
- Sexual abuse
- Loss of a loved one
- Infertility
- Medical illness
- Witnessing a trauma
- Experiencing a trauma
- New job
- Chronic pain
- Chronic stress
- Empty nest
- Life transitions
- Retirement
- A combination of events

Going through major life transitions is difficult enough without a bout of depression. When you go through a life event, turn to your treatment team to help you navigate your way through it.

Group 5:
Depression and Life Events (Cont...)

STAYING STUCK CAN FEED DEPRESSION
In her book Frequency, Penny Pierce (2009) describes how we can create a state of being stuck and feeling like we can't move forward with our lives. This feeling of being stuck can exacerbate feelings of depression.
She describes the following ways of feeling stuck:

- You've finished a chapter in your life and you refuse to let go of it. You hold on to it by self-criticism, fear, failure, and a sense that life is rejecting you.

- You want something so badly that you spend your time and energy trying to force it to happen. You live in a state of complaining and protesting where your life is at.

- An experience triggers a past memory. You go back to living in the past and getting into a state of self-blame and control.

- You live in a state of focusing on what you do not have, what you may never have, or who you may never be. You live in an empty reality and can't move forward.

- You're so attached to your habits and current identity that you live in a holding pattern. You live in a holding pattern fueled by old beliefs, holding back the truth, and convincing yourself that you can't move forward.

- You're drained from too much negativity, conflict, and willfulness.
  Too much stress and lack of energy keep you from moving forward.

  Some other forms of feeling stuck could have their origin in:
  - You are trying to make a big life decision and you feel like you live in a state of tug of war. One day you are pulled this way and the next day you are pulled the other way. Living on this see-saw will keep you living in your own pain.

  - You are fearful and afraid to live out of your authentic self. If there is an important piece of you that you work hard at keeping hidden (sexual identity, working in a career you don't enjoy, and so on) it can trigger major depression. As long as you choose to keep this piece of you hidden from others you will feel depressed.

Organizations to Get to Know

There are several good groups dedicated to helping individuals who suffer from depression.

NAMI – National Alliance on Mental Illness
This group is the nation's largest grassroots mental health organization dedicated to helping those who are living with mental illness.
Their hotline number is 800-950-6264 and their website is www.nami.org.

DBSA – Depression and Bipolar Support Alliance
Their mission is to provide hope, help, and support to improve the lives of people who have mood disorders.
Their number is 800-826-3632 and their website is www.dbsaalliance.org.

NATIONAL SUICIDE PREVENTION HOTLINE - 800-273-8255
This hotline provides 24 hour, toll-free availability to anyone in a suicidal crisis or distress.

YOUR LOCAL GROUPS
It's also very important to find out what crisis hotlines and mental health groups exist in your local area before you need to access them. Your local crisis hotline number is _____

■ **GROUP EXERCISE 1:**
Feeling Stuck – Journal about any area in your life that you are feeling stuck and how it relates to your moods.

_____

_____

_____

_____

_____

■ **GROUP EXERCISE 2:**
Depression Timeline – Map out or make a timeline of depression throughout your life.

"Depression is a prison where you are both the suffering prisoner and the critical jailer"

- Dorothy Rowe -

Group 6:
Meditation and Depression

People are now turning to meditation to help manage many different health issues. Studies are showing some mixed results on its effectiveness to help manage depression. Some are having success combining mindfulness with Cognitive Behavioral Therapy and are calling it MCBT. While studies are showing promising results, the best news is that meditation has no harmful side-effects and has many health benefits.

LEARNING TO BE MINDFUL
Mindfulness is a conscious willingness to observe what you are doing in any given moment of your life. Jon Kabat-Zinn, a thought leader in mindfulness education, defines mindfulness as "the intentional, accepting, non-judgmental focus of one's attention on the emotions, thoughts, and sensations occurring in the present moment."

In a nutshell, mindfulness is –
- Start Observing Your Thoughts
- Stop Judging Your Thoughts
- Stillness & Silence / Living in the moment

Learning to start observing your thoughts is a very helpful tool. When you keep thinking about "what if this happens" or "everything could go wrong" or so many other catastrophic thoughts, depressive thoughts are not far behind. Changing or reframing your thoughts is one of the goals of cognitive behavioral therapy.

To stop judging your thoughts is also a helpful tool when dealing with depression. When you judge your thoughts you can end up feeling less than or ashamed of yourself. Always remember that depression has a voice of its own. Practice letting these thoughts go and choosing more positive ones to focus on.

Practicing stillness and quiet is good for everyone's mind as it produces a sense of relaxation. Living in the present moment keeps you from the pain of your past and from worrying about the future.

GatheringForGroups.com

Group 6:
Meditation and Depression (Cont...)

PRACTICING BEING MINDFUL
One way to begin practicing paying attention to your thoughts is to sit quietly and just observe what thoughts are going through your mind. This may feel a little awkward at first, as our culture doesn't make or take much time to sit quietly with ourselves. For your first meditation try and sit quietly for 10 minutes. Try not to think about things you feel you need to be getting done, just relax.

As thoughts drift in and out (and they will) of your mind, don't pass judgment on them, just let them sail by. One easy way to clear your mind is to close your eyes and only pay attention to your breathing. Give your full attention to it and don't focus on anything else. Paying attention to your breathing and how your chest and stomach expand as you breathe will hopefully put you into a more relaxed state. It's during this quiet, very relaxed state your inner voice speaks to you providing insights into your life. As you continue to practice meditation, try and build up to 15-20 minutes and see how you feel.

Another good way to learn to meditate is to download free guided meditations on-line. These meditations have someone's soothing voice guiding you through a relaxing process. As your mind focuses on his/her voice, your competing thoughts for your attention seem to disappear.

MIND-BODY CONNECTION
You've no doubt experienced a gut feeling about a situation and either chose to ignore it or to go with it. Often times you found out that your gut feeling was a wise one and that going with it paid off. Our bodies speak to us all day long. Paying attention to these physical sensations is one more tool for tuning into your emotions.

Depression is often accompanied by crying, body aches, and other physical symptoms. If you notice body responses while meditating, don't be afraid. Whatever comes up in your body is just what it is meant to be. Go with these responses and embrace them instead of being afraid of them and trying to stop them. Perhaps your mind and inner voice will share an insight about your depression with you.

Group 6:
Meditation and Depression (Cont...)

BODY SCAN

To become more familiar with where your body stores depression, you can learn to do a body scan. The body scan is a simple, progressive, slow method for paying attention to any tension you are carrying from your head to your toes. Take a minute or two and get relaxed. Starting with your head, ask yourself what sensations you feel in this part of your body. Focus on sensations, instead of emotions. For example, notice any tightness or shallow breathing, or muscle pain and so forth in each area of your body. You'll notice your body's sensations are connected to your emotions. For example, when you're angry you'll probably feel your muscles getting tighter and your breathing a little shallower. Next time you meditate, practice doing a body scan before and afterwards. See if your body reveals anything to you regarding your depressed state.

■ **GROUP EXERCISE 1:**
Body Scan and Visualization

_____

_____

_____

■ **GROUP EXERCISE 2:**
Mindfulness Meditation

_____

_____

_____

According to the World Health Organization fact sheet on depression,

"Globally, more than 350 million people of all ages suffer from depression."

Closing Thoughts

Hopefully your group experience has encouraged you and strengthened you in some way. Perhaps listening to other's stories and experiences with their depression has given you some new perspectives. Maybe you learned some new coping skills. Most likely your insights and ideas have inspired other members in the group. As you leave the group always remember:

- 350 Million people suffer from depression. You are not alone.
- Sadness, Situational, and Clinical depression are all different.
- Assessments are available to help you identify your depression.
- Every type of depression affects you mentally, physically, emotionally, and spiritually.
- Assemble a team of health care professionals, family members, and friends to help you manage your depression.
- Researchers are exploring more definitive reasons for what causes depression. Keep up on the latest research and developments.
- Don't let myths about depression bring you down or keep you from seeking the help you need.
- There's many treatment options available. Put together a plan that works for you.
- Don't try and meet any family or friend's expectations you find difficult when you are going through a bout of depression.
- Be aware that when you are going through a major life event, depression can show up and make its presence known.
- Put your local crisis hotline number in your cell phone in case you need it for you or someone else.
- Settling down the mind helps to settle down the body.
- Never give up or give in…no matter how bad your depression gets.

Your Closing Thoughts

You've spent the past few weeks exploring facets of your depression. Describe any ways being in the group has affected how you will deal with your depression.

References

World Health Organization Depression Fact Sheet (October 2012)
http://www.who.int/mediacentre/factsheets/fs369/en/

Holmes, Lindsay (2015, December) 11 Statistics that will change your mind about depression. The Huffington Post. www.huffingtonpost.com

The National Institute of Mental Health (May, 2015) Depression.
http://nimh.nih.gov/health/topics/depression/index.shtml.

Pierce, Penny (2009) Frequency- the Power of Personal Vibration pp. 80-82. Beyond Words Publishing, Inc.

Goyal, M. MD, MPH, Singh, S. MD, MPH, et al..Meditation Programs for Psychological Stress and Well-being. (March 2014) JAMA.

Notes

www.ingramcontent.com/pod-product-compliance
Lightning Source LLC
LaVergne TN
LVHW081526060526
838200LV00044B/2014